RIVER
JOURNEYS

THE THAMES

DAVID CUMMING

Wayland

RIVER JOURNEYS

The Ganges
The Thames
The Amazon
The Nile

Main cover: An aerial view of the Thames at Tower Bridge in London.

Series editor: Deb Elliott
Series designer: Malcolm Walker
Cover designer: Simon Balley

Text is based on *The Thames* in the World's Rivers series published in 1993.

First published in 1995 by
Wayland (Publishers) Limited
61 Western Road, Hove
East Sussex BN3 1JD, England

British Library Cataloguing in Publication Data
Cumming, David
 Thames. - (River Journeys Series)
 I. Title   II. Series
 942.2

 ISBN 0–75021422 8

Typeset in the UK by Kudos
Printed and bound in Italy by G. Canale C.S.p.A.

Contents

The Thames

The Thames is the best-known river in Britain, even though it is not very long. Once it was important for transport and trade. Today it is used more for pleasure. Farmers also need water from the Thames for their animals and crops.

This map shows the route of the Thames across Britain. ▶

The sun sets behind Tower Bridge in London, the most famous bridge across the Thames. ▼

Along the river

The Thames is only 352 km long, so it is a very small river compared to the River Nile (6,695 km) in Africa or the River Amazon (6,570 km) in South America.

The Thames starts at a spring, called Thameshead, in a field in Gloucestershire. The spring is supplied by water from deep under the ground.

The spring at the start of the River Thames in Gloucestershire makes the ground muddy. ▼

▲ *The Thames twists and turns through the countryside to the west of London.*

No one is exactly sure how old the Thames is, but people think it has existed for more than 30 million years.

It has changed its route many times over the centuries. Today, many smaller rivers, called tributaries, join the Thames on its journey from Gloucestershire to the North Sea.

Rain falling on to land drains away into the rivers flowing through it. The area of land drained by a river and its tributaries is called its drainage basin. Most of southern England is part of the River Thames's drainage basin. Any rain falling on it ends up in the Thames, which takes it to the sea.

This map shows the Thames's drainage basin – the area of southern England drained by the Thames and its tributaries. ▼

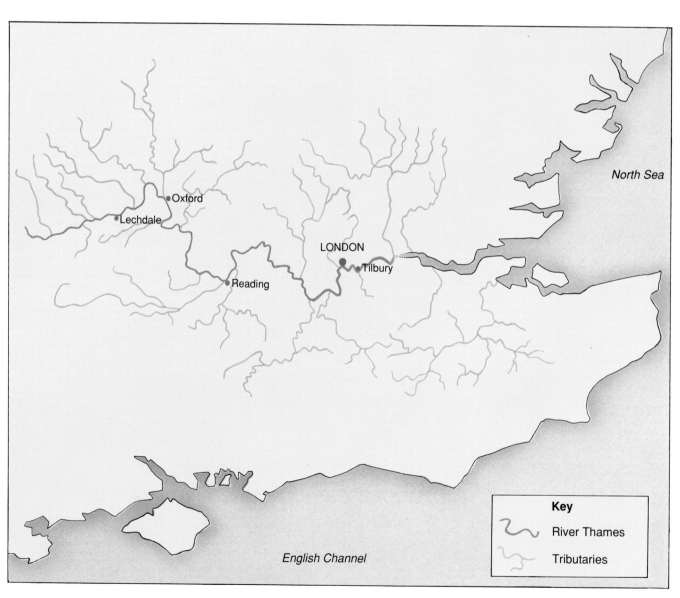

North Sea

Oxford
Lechdale
LONDON
Tilbury
Reading

English Channel

Key

River Thames

Tributaries

▲ *The Thames flowing through the centre of London.*

◄ *The muddy mouth of the Thames in the North Sea.*

9

◄ *This is the weir at Marlow. You can see where Marlow is on the map on page 5.*

This is the gate of the lock on the Thames at Teddington. ▶

Weirs (like small dams) have been built along the Thames near places where the river is shallow. The weirs make the water deeper so that boats can use it. Locks are another way of making sure that the river is deep enough for boats.

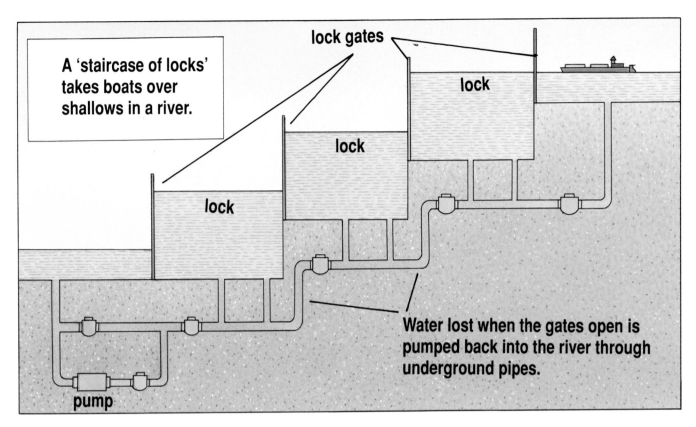

A 'staircase of locks' takes boats over shallows in a river.

lock gates

lock

lock

lock

lock

Water lost when the gates open is pumped back into the river through underground pipes.

pump

▲ This diagram shows how a lock works.

The locks can raise or lower boats along a watery 'staircase' of steps to avoid shallow places.

◀ Land near the Thames has often been flooded by the river when there has been too much water in it.

11

This man is in charge of the 80 people who work on the Thames Barrier in London.

The barrier was built in 1982 to stop water from the North Sea going up the Thames and flooding London.

Strong winds can blow sea water up the Thames and cause dangerous floods. In 1953 a bad storm pushed a lot of sea water into the mouth of the Thames and 300 people were drowned.

This is the Thames Barrier.

Sometimes the barrier will not shut properly because of all the mud on the bottom of the river. The mud has to be cleared before the barrier will close.

Past times

Archaeologists have found things in the ground which show that people were living by the River Thames 300,000 years ago. These people sharpened stones to use as knives and as axes to cut down trees in the forests along the river banks.

After digging at this place near the Thames, archaeologists found the sharpened stone on the right. ▼

13

This clay jug was made by people who lived near the Thames long before the Celts arrived in Britain.

The Celts

About 2,500 years ago the Celts, a people from Europe, invaded southern Britain. They crossed the English Channel in ships, some of which went up the Thames.

The Celts conquered the local peoples and then built forts to protect themselves. The remains of some of these forts can be seen today.

This shield belonged to a Celt soldier. It was found on the bottom of the Thames. ▶

14

Part of a statue of the Roman Emperor Hadrian which was found in the Thames. ▶

The Romans

Nearly 2,000 years ago the Celts were attacked from Europe by the Romans. Soon the Roman emperors ruled all of England and Wales.

The Romans were the first people to make good use of the Thames. They built big barges to travel along it, and harbours where the boats could be loaded with cargoes. The Romans also built the first bridge across the river.

This castle in Rochester, Kent, was built by the Normans who came to Britain after the Romans. ▶

Saxons and Vikings

About 1,600 years ago the Romans were attacked and defeated by the Saxons from northern Europe. The Saxons built many villages along the Thames. Any town or village whose name ends with 'ing', like Reading, has been around since Saxon times.

Nearly 1,200 years ago the Saxons were conquered by the Vikings from Scandinavia. The Viking king, Cnut (or Canute) became the ruler of Britain.

The Normans

The Normans, from France, were the last people to invade Britain. They defeated the Saxon army in 1066 at the Battle of Hastings. Their leader, William the Conqueror, became the King of Britain.

William the Conqueror built many castles by the Thames, including the ones at Windsor, Wallingford and Rochester (see the photograph on page 15). You can find these places on the map on page 5.

This is the Tower of London, which is in the castle built by William the Conqueror beside the Thames in London. It was once a prison where criminals would be taken by boat through the entrance marked 'Traitors' Gate'. Today, the British queen's crown jewels are kept in the Tower, guarded by men called 'Beefeaters'.

Winters used to be much colder in Britain and there would be ice on the River Thames. The ice would be thick enough for carriages and people to go on without cracking.

Winter fairs, like this one, would be held on the Thames when it froze. The last fair took place in 1814.

River transport

The first boats on the Thames were tree trunks tied together to make rafts. The rafts were used for carrying passengers and cargoes along the river. Later, tree trunks were hollowed out to make canoes in which people could sit. The canoes were used for catching fish.

▼ *Ships and boats on the Thames at Greenwich in the 1700s.*

▲ *Large sailing boats used to carry cargoes along the Thames.*

Before engines were invented, river boats were driven by oars and sails or pulled along by teams of horses or men walking beside the river. Sometimes as many as 80 strong men would be needed to pull a heavy boat full of cargo.

In the days before good roads and railways, heavy cargoes were transported by water. Long, thin, flat-bottomed boats, called barges, were built to carry the cargoes. With their flat bottoms, the barges could travel along canals and rivers because they did not need deep water.

Many modern barges have their own engines, but some are pushed or pulled by tug-boats.

These barges have no engines, so they are being pulled down the Thames by a powerful tug-boat. ▼

▲ *Tilbury harbour, near the mouth of the Thames.*

Barges brought cargoes to London from all over Britain. They would travel down canals to the Thames and then along the river to the city.

Some of these cargoes would be loaded on to ships in London's harbours and taken to other countries. In 1866 a new harbour was built at Tilbury, 40 km from London. It soon became the most important harbour on the river.

Tilbury is on the mouth of the Thames, so it can be used by big ships which cannot reach the harbours in London. As a result the London harbours have been shut and the land used for new offices and homes. Many of the ships using Tilbury today carry their cargoes in large metal boxes, called containers. The containers are easy to load and unload, so they save time and money.

This photograph was taken in 1962. Since then this London harbour has been closed. ▶

◀ *Because there are no harbours, there are more tourist boats than barges on the Thames.*

This is Paul Brookes, the captain of the *Abercorn*, a passenger boat which can carry 276 people.

Paul takes tourists along the Thames in London to show them all the interesting places.

The *Abercorn* was built in 1924 but it is still in good working order. It has been used in films.

Cargoes are now transported by trains and trucks, so there are few barges on the Thames. Most of the boats on it are used for carrying tourists. Others are used for parties and have restaurants and discos.

On an evening in 1989, this disco river boat was hit by a ship and it sank. Fifty people died.

This was the biggest disaster since 1878, when two steamers crashed and 640 people were drowned.

River crossings

Before bridges, people used to cross the Thames at fords. These were places where the water was shallow enough to walk across to the opposite bank.

This bridge at Newbridge, near Oxford, was built in the 1400s. It is one of the oldest on the Thames. ▼

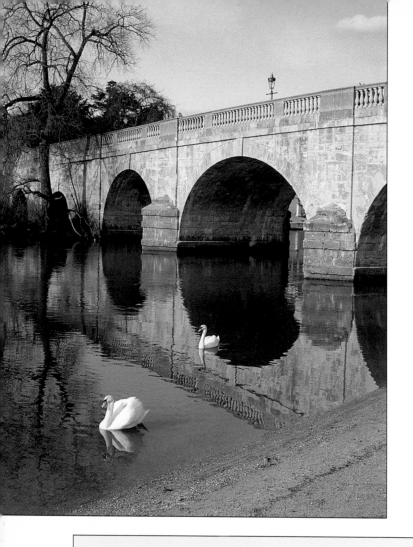

◄ We know the places where people once crossed the river because they have 'ford' in their names. This is the bridge at Wallingford.

The first bridge across the Thames was built by the Romans in London. It was made of wood. London was the capital city of Roman Britain. The Romans called it Londinium.

London Bridge

In 1209 a stone bridge replaced the Romans' wooden bridge in London. It had taken 33 years to finish. Although it was only 6 m wide, shops and houses were built on it, as this picture shows.

There was a drawbridge in the middle which could be raised to allow sailing ships to pass through.

Tower Bridge, in London, was opened in 1894. Its two towers are over 60 m high. ▶

In the days when there were few bridges in London, 'watermen' would ferry people across the Thames in rowing-boats. Very rich people had their own boats to take them to the other side, so they did not use the watermen.

▼ *The Thames's newest bridge, opened at Dartford in 1991.*

27

◄ *This small ferry carries people between Windsor and Eton, towns on opposite banks of the Thames.*

In 1842 the first tunnel under the Thames was opened at Rotherhithe. Since then many other tunnels have been built to carry trains, people or traffic beneath the river.

This diagram shows where all the tunnels and bridges in London cross the River Thames. ▼

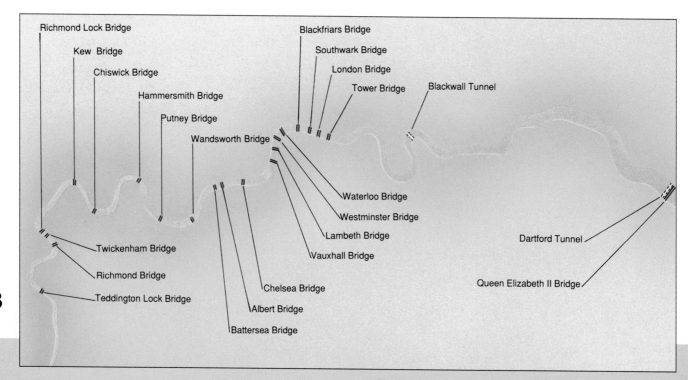

Richmond Lock Bridge

Kew Bridge

Chiswick Bridge

Hammersmith Bridge

Putney Bridge

Wandsworth Bridge

Blackfriars Bridge

Southwark Bridge

London Bridge

Tower Bridge

Blackwall Tunnel

Twickenham Bridge

Richmond Bridge

Teddington Lock Bridge

Waterloo Bridge

Westminster Bridge

Lambeth Bridge

Vauxhall Bridge

Chelsea Bridge

Albert Bridge

Battersea Bridge

Dartford Tunnel

Queen Elizabeth II Bridge

Farming

The earliest people who lived by the Thames hunted, fished and gathered fruits and berries in the forests along the river's banks.

People began to farm the Thames about 6,500 years ago. They knew how to sharpen stones to make axes with which they could cut down the forests for fields. They grew wheat in the fields, as well as keeping cattle and sheep there.

The first farmers lived in round houses like this one. The walls were made of dried mud. The roof was made with branches from trees covered with thatch. There was only one door and no windows.

Farming along the Thames has changed little over the centuries. The main difference is that fields have got bigger and bigger as small farms have been bought by owners of larger farms next to them.

In the western areas of the Thames, most of the land is used for sheep. There are fewer sheep now than in the Middle Ages, when wool was important to Britain's trade with Europe.

▼ *Cattle grazing by the Thames in Oxfordshire.*

Stephen Cook is a farmer by the Thames. He grows wheat, oil seed and hay on his land. He also keeps cattle in the fields by the side of the river, where the ground is too wet to grow any crops.

In the eastern areas of the Thames, farmers grow a lot of cereal crops, like wheat and barley, in their fields.

◄ *In the Middle Ages there were more sheep by the Thames than today.*

31

Towns and cities

Many towns and cities have been built along the Thames because people need water to live.

◀ *The university in Oxford.*

▲ *Abingdon was once important because of its church.*

Oxford is the first city on the Thames as you travel down the river from its start. It gets its name from the ford which oxen could use to cross the river. Oxford is now famous for its university, which is the oldest in Britain.

Down the river from Oxford is the town of Abingdon. It had one of the most important and richest churches in Britain. But the church was closed by King Henry VIII in the 1530s, along with many other churches in Britain.

◀ *Rowers on the Thames at the town of Henley.*

People come from all over the world to visit Windsor Castle, near the Thames. ▶

Just before London is Windsor. This small town grew up around the castle that was built by the Normans in 1070. The castle has been changed many times since then.

Windsor Castle is the biggest in the world and is still used by the royal family. After the Tower of London, the castle is the most popular place on the Thames for people to visit.

London is the largest city on the Thames. Nearly 7 million people live there.

The government of Britain has its offices in London and makes new laws in the Houses of Parliament by the side of the river. Parliament's clock tower is the famous Big Ben.

London is full of theatres, cinemas, art galleries and restaurants, which thousands of people visit very day. Many of them are on holiday from other countries.

▲ *This is the Tate Galley in London, which is full of many famous paintings.*

◄ *The Houses of Parliament and Big Ben by the Thames in London.*

35

Industries

In the Middle Ages fishing was an important business on the Thames. Many types of fish, including salmon, cod, and herring, were caught and then sold in markets.

▼ *Fishing on the Thames is now a hobby, not a business.*

▲ *The Thames and its tributaries are much cleaner today than they were ten years ago.*

In the 1800s dirty water from factories and homes began to pollute the river badly. Soon no fish could live in the Thames and the fishing industry finished.

The Thames is cleaner now because the government has made new laws forbidding dirty water being put into the river. Fish are starting to come back to live in the river and anglers are catching them for fun and not for business.

▲ *Ships bring oil to this refinery at the mouth of the Thames The refinery turns the oil into petrol.*

There are many different industries along the Thames. Most of the big factories are to be found between London and the mouth of the Thames.

Tourism is one of the most important industries. People come from all over the world to visit places like Oxford and Windsor. They spend a lot of money in shops, hotels and restaurants.

In London, many firms make money from buying and selling things. ▶

Many tourists visit Hampton Court when they stay in London. ▶

39

Pollution

In the 1800s most of the drinking water for London came from the Thames. The water was not cleaned before it was pumped to homes and offices.

◀ This picture from 1844 shows dirty water being emptied straight into a tributary of the Thames in London.

Thames water is cleaned in these special ponds before being sent by pipes to homes, offices and schools. ▶

In 1832, 5,300 people in London died from cholera, an illness which is caused by germs in dirty water. In the 1840s, 1850s and 1860s thousands more died from the illness.

It was decided to build 'treatment plants', where river water for London would be cleaned before it was sent to homes. The treatment plants also cleaned dirty water from homes before it went back into the Thames.

During the Second World War (1939–45) many treatment plants and water pipes were damaged by German bombs. A lot of dirty water went into the Thames and killed the fish and plants living in it.

New treatment plants and pipes were built in the 1950s. In the 1960s new laws were made to stop factories letting their dirty water go into the river.

Drinking water
Every day 4,500 million litres of clean drinking water are pumped from the Thames along 42,000 km of pipes to homes, offices, schools, factories and hospitals.

These new businesses must be careful about emptying dirty water into the river. ▶

Here are some of the birds and fish you will see today on a journey along the River Thames. ▼

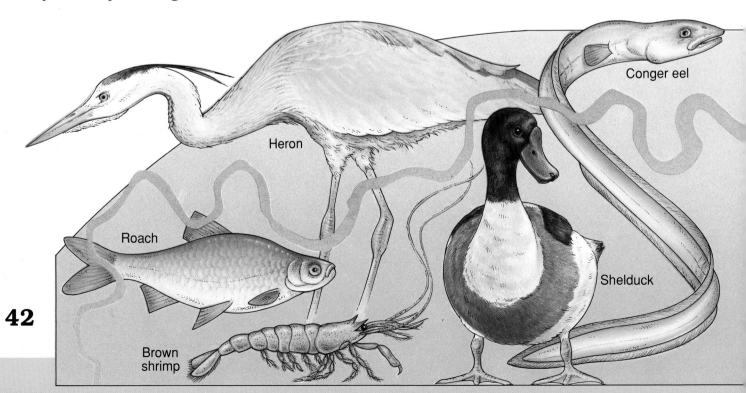

Heron

Conger eel

Roach

Shelduck

Brown shrimp

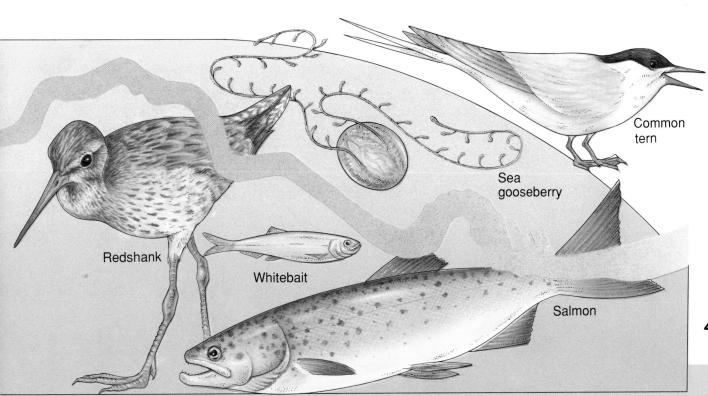

Redshank

Whitebait

Salmon

Sea gooseberry

Common tern

43

Today the Thames is cleaner than it has been for a very long time, and over 109 different types of fish live in it.

This is Alan Cooper. He works as a scientist for the National Rivers Authority.

Every week Alan travels along the Thames in a boat to test the water's dirtiness. He makes a special check of water near factories and treatment plants. He uses his laboratory on the boat to see if there are any poisonous chemicals in water.

Although less dirty water goes into the river from homes and factories, many poisonous chemicals drain into it from farmers' fields. The chemicals come from the fertilizers and pesticides used by farmers on their crops.

In the future the government hopes farmers will use less chemicals so that the River Thames will not be harmed.

The future

In the past the Thames was important for transporting cargoes. Few cargo boats use it now because London's docks have been shut and there are good roads and railways.

In the future the Thames will be used a lot for pleasure. People will visit all the famous cities and buildings on its banks. They will walk alongside it, fish or swim in it, or sail boats on it.

Hopefully, everyone will enjoy the Thames without harming it.

▼ *A quiet evening on the River Thames.*

45

Glossary

archaeologist A person who studies old buildings and things found in the ground.

art gallery A building where people go to look at paintings and sculptures.

barge A flat-bottomed boat used for carrying cargoes along rivers and canals.

cargo Goods carried in a ship, truck, train or plane.

centuries Hundreds of years.

cereals The name for crops like wheat, rye, barley and oats.

crops Something grown by farmers for food.

crown jewels The special jewels worn when someone is made king or queen.

fertilizer Something given to crops to help them to grow better.

harbour A place where cargo can be put on or taken off ships.

invade **To** attack a land or an area which is not your own.

laboratory A room or building in which scientists work.

lock Part of a river or canal that may be closed off with gates so that boats can be raised or lowered across shallow water.

Middle Ages The years in history from 1100 to 1500.

mouth The place where a river widens as it enters the sea.

pesticides Chemicals that kill insects which harm crops.

pollution Harming the environment, for example by letting chemicals and dirty water go into a river.

spring A place where water comes out of the ground.

tourist Someone on holiday.

tributaries Small rivers that flow into a large one.

weir A small dam built across a river to make it deeper.

Books to read

A Journey Down the Thames by Laurie Bolwell (Wayland, 1983)

Picture acknowledgements
All pictures are by Isabel Lilly except the following: Cephas/Nigel Blythe 4, 27 (top); C.M.Dixon 13 (both), 14 (both), 15 (top), 23 (top), 29; © Michael Holford 25; Hulton Picture Co. 11; The Image Bank left panel, cover (A. T. Willett); Tony Stone Worldwide main cover (Pritchard); Topham 20, 21, 24 (lower); Wayland Picture Library 18, 19, 26 (lower), 40. The map on page 5 is by Peter Bull Design. The artwork on pages 8, 11, 28 and 42-3 is by John Yates.

Index